I0435942

Relationships:

Dress Like You Have Inside Information

Catherine E. Storing

The Confidence Building Coach Co.

www.StylingFaith.Com

Also by Catherine E. Storing

Dream Big: Seven Keys to Stepping Into Your Calling

Styling Faith: The Complete Style Guide

The Organized Closet: From Disaster Zone to Fabulous with my 20 Oh-So-Simple Steps!

Soñando En Mayuscula

Confidence: 8 Bold Steps to Arrive to Your Calling in Style!

Copyright

I dedicate this book to everyone waiting for the mate God has set aside for him or her; waiting on Him is the best thing we could ever do.

Content

This content was previously presented live at the First Church of Periscope Relationship Retreat in Atlanta, GA 3/19/2016.

This content is based on Jeremiah 29:11 (Amp Bible)

For I know the plans and thoughts that I have for you,' says the Lord, 'plans for peace and wellbeing and not for disaster to give you a future and a hope.

About the Author.

I am Catherine Storing, a fashion stylist, a confidence-building coach and a woman of faith. I am all three at the same time because I don't want to and I don't have to choose. I help women and a few brave men to look good from the inside out, so they can do what they have been called to do while looking all kinds of fine.

I am also a speaker and an author. I just gave my first *TEDx* talk: Meaningful Beauty is an Inside Job - hbit.ly/meaningful-talk. It was my first, and I believe it is going to the first of many. I have written four books. My bestseller is *Styling Faith: The Complete Style Guide.* It is a complete guide because I threw in everything I know about style and everything else.

Some people are called to be a little bit of salt in the world. That is not me. I was *not* called to be a little bit of salt. I am a business owner, but I am a woman of God before anything else. Before I am a woman, I am a person of God, first and foremost. I am an over-the-top kind of girl because I have an over-the-top kind of God. I am all kinds of fine all the time because I know whose I am, and I know what I am supposed to be doing. I am on assignment and my assignment requires me to look all kinds of fine – #pureandfine. And it is possible. It is doable. I do it every day. You can be pure and fine too.

You can find me at www.stylingfaith.com or www.catherinestoring.com.

Relationships: Dress Like You Have Inside Information.

What I want to share with you about relationships is Bible inspired. Everything I teach, even the style part, I get from the Bible.

The title of this book is Relationships: *Dress like You Have Inside Information.* And you *do* have to dress like you have inside information. I know what many of you are thinking, "Catherine, what on earth does how you dress have to do with relationships?"

Don't worry; I am going to explain why how you dress has a great deal to do with relationships.

Today, many people, unfortunately, are getting divorced. Your relationships are not working out and things are ending *not* because you aren't happy. Things are ending and you are having trouble with your partner *not* because you are not trying hard enough. *The reason relationships are not working out is because we have forgotten we have inside information.* There is work to be done before you get in a relationship. That is the plain and simple truth.

There is work to be done and unfortunately, we rush in and forget we have inside information.

Right now, you may be thinking, "Catherine, I don't have inside information. Maybe *you* got the memo. Maybe *you* got the download. Perhaps God sent you a text with inside information, but I seem to have missed out."

He gave it to you too. He has given you the inside information and you have just forgotten. But don't worry – I am here to take care of you. I am going to remind you what the inside information is and when you remember, it is going to transform your life. You have heard this before, but you have not heard it the way you are going to hear it today – not because the way I am going to say it is any different, but because the Holy Spirit is right here. He is here and He is going to open your mind and your understanding so you can comprehend on a new level. You will hear so deeply that your mind will become new. His Word is good and his mercies are new every single day. What is the inside information? I am going to tell you.

Let us look at Jeremiah 29:11, from the Amplified Version. We are going to take it in bite size pieces because sometimes we get overwhelmed, take things for granted and don't realize that in a few words there is a lot of content. There is a lot of blessing in a few words.

So this is the beginning, just the very beginning. *"For I know the plans and thoughts that I have for you..."*

That right there is the beginning of your inside information. My sisters and my brothers, if we would remember this scripture, we would not rush to just take anything that comes our way. We would not hurry towards good enough. We would not settle for, "Well, he believes in God. He has heard the name of Jesus." "She is really fine, but her spirituality is not quite on point, but you know what, she is here now."

I am getting old and I have heard all the excuses. "If I don't grab this, maybe nobody else is going to come along."

Have you said that to yourself? It applies to everything – to relationships, to jobs, to businesses, to opportunities, to everything. "I am not going to get this chance again. This is all I am going to get."

Oh my goodness. I have to remind you that Jeremiah 29:11 says, *"For I know the plans and the thoughts that I have about you."* That isn't Catherine Storing saying that. What does the scripture say? *"So says the Lord."* He is not a man that he should lie. So if He says, *"I know the plans and the thoughts I have for you,"* He's got it. You can breathe. If you have troubles right now – if you have debt, if you have problems, if your business is not growing, if your husband is giving you a really hard time, or if your wife is spending too much and she is not listening to you – I want you to remember that He's got it. It is already done. It is finished, so you can breathe.

Last night, I slept like a big baby with a clean diaper and I was as happy as a clam because I knew that He had it. I knew I was empty. I gave everything I needed to give during the day and I received so much back because I did not settle for being a Christian who has a little bit of salt. I am an over-the-top kind of Christian because I have been given so much. Why would I keep all those blessings to myself? We have the antidote. People are dying next to you and you are not telling them what they need.

"Catherine, what does that have to do with relationship? What does that have to do with dressing like you have inside information?"

Well, let me explain. My business and my calling is styling faith – a faith which changes and transforms from the inside out. Do you think I look good just to look good? That is not what I am doing; I am not that shallow. I am dressing the part because I am on a job, I am on assignment. I have to make it easy for people to listen to me. I know you are saying, "Catherine, that's not the way it works."

But yes, it does work that way because we judge people. Attractive people get away with a lot. You know that is true. People are going to let pretty people cut in line. I know because I do it all the time. I do it all the time because I have favor, and I activate that favor by believing it is going to be there. I ask for favor and then I don't worry about it. I remember I am on assignment. He's got it and He has provided everything I need.

So, you are in a relationship or you are about to enter a relationship. Remember, everything is a relationship. Maybe you are divorced. Maybe you are a widower. Maybe you are saying, "I swore off relationships. I am not going to look for anybody."

Everything is a relationship. Even when you get your coffee at Starbucks, you have a relationship with your barista. They have to get your coffee right, on time, make sure it is hot, and the type you ordered. You want mocha with skim and Equal or Splenda. You want half of this and half of that. You know what I am talking about. Many of you have a very complicated order so you want the barista to get it right.

So, why on earth would you dress in a way that is going to attract the wrong person? We do this all the time. The people I have in my life reflects on me. If we are related, if you are hanging out with me, you cannot look all kinds of crazy. I won't stand for that. That is not okay. It is not okay to look like a ragamuffin with your hair messed up and paint stains on your clothes. "Oh maybe when I paint my house again, I'll need that outfit."

Are you kidding me? When I paint, I don't get paint all over me. When I have to go out and take care of things, I am not going to put on ugly clothes. Why would I do that? My body is the temple of the Holy Spirit. Why on earth would I not take care of myself 24/7?

Let's talk about outside because I have seen some things I wish I could un-see. Have you seen those videos from people at Wal-Mart? It is not a joke. People aren't just dressing like that for the camera. No! People go out like that. And then they wonder, "Why are the low lies, the non-quality people hitting on me? Why do I have friends who are not quality people?"

Remember, everything is a relationship. Everything!

There are people who won't talk to me and I am okay with that. I thank them because I know we don't have anything in common. What would we talk about? If you are not reading the Bible, if you are not in the Word, if you are not looking upwards, if you are not thinking everything is going to work out in your favor and more, then we have nothing to talk about. We are not at the same level. I am not earth-minded, I am heaven-minded. That means the people I talk to have to be heaven-minded. And they have to look the part because they know Whose they are. They know what they are about, their calling and their purpose. So your outfit, what you put on your body, has to match and represent the person you are. And remember, *"I know the plans and the thoughts I have for you,"* says the Lord.

The next part of Jeremiah 29:11 says, *"Plans for peace."* Perhaps you feel sometimes that you have no peace. That is not the legacy or the thoughts God has for you. He has thoughts of peace for you, and that extends to your relationships. If you have no peace in your life, there is something wrong. God is not in your union. God is not in your relationship. There are some things you have to change. "But Catherine, my spouse is not reading this. My wife is not reading this. My brother is not reading this – they need to hear this."

Honey, darling, I love you. *You* need to hear this. That is why are reading this. You need to hear this because everything starts with you. You cannot change anybody else and you know you have tried. I know I have tried. It doesn't work. It just doesn't. You have to change yourself. You are the only person you can change.

If you have issues with a lot of people – and I know many of you do because in the past, I did too – and the people are different but you are the same, then *you* are the common denominator. If you don't change, you are going to continue getting the same results.

If you have no peace in your life, what are you bringing to your relationships? What attitude, what thoughts, and what actions are you bringing to all your relationships which are not in line with God's will, or the person you were created to be? You were created to be someone amazing. Don't kick yourself. And don't think that because you have done some things and been some places that you can't be amazing. Remember, your past qualifies you. When you have done crazy stuff, God glorifies Himself even more. If you have no peace, you have to remember the thoughts and the plans God has for you and one of them is peace.

What is the next part? This is one of my favorites – "*And well-being.*" Oh my goodness! "*And well-being...*"

How are your relationships right now? Do you have drama in your life? Ask yourself – "Do I have drama in my life right now? How is my business? How is my job? How is my house looking? How is my car? Is the area where I work chaotic?"

If the answer is yes, you are out of alignment. There is something missing if you don't have well-being in your life. You have to go back and read this over and over again until it enters your head and your heart, and it stays there. *"He has a thought and plan for your peace and well-being."*

I don't know about you but that sentence makes me feel good. I find peace right there when I know He is the God Almighty and He has a thought and a plan about me for peace and well-being. And you have to accept that. Many of you have a hard time accepting gifts.

I often teach people how to accept a compliment and how to give them. Many people don't know how to do that. A compliment is a gift and many of you are very rude. I want you to stop it. If I say, "Oh my, gosh! I love your hair," some people will respond with every reason why their hair is not nice.

"Oh, do you see this or did you see that?"

My answer is always, "No."

So, I stop people now. I say, "Wait a second. Let's try that one more time. Maybe what you meant to say was, 'Thank you, Catherine.'"

And I have them repeat that back to me. They have to repeat it because I need to know they understand.

When I teach people how to receive a compliment, I give them my script. I give them permission to steal it, borrow it, whatever they want, because my script changes lives. It took me years to perfect it, and I am going to give it to you because you are not receiving in your relationships. Someone is trying to give you something – their love, their attention, money, gifts – and you are just being flat-out rude. You need to change that and stop right now.

This is what I do when somebody pays me a compliment. The first thing they usually notice is my hair. "Oh my goodness! I love your hair. It is so red. It is so bright. I love that. I love your curls."

When I go to the airport, to the grocery store, to get gas, wherever I am going, I get compliments. When I do, I look the person in the eye, smile my biggest smile, open my big brown eyes, hold my heart, and say, "Oh my goodness! Thank you so much. I really, really appreciate that," and I stop speaking.

That is what you have to do. It is that simple. Do you know why I hold my heart? It is because I want to make sure they know I am receiving what they are saylng, that I am taking their gift inside my chest. It is not going to my head. I am not getting a big head because I received a compliment. I take it into my heart and say, "Wow! Thank you so much. I really appreciate that."

And I stop. I don't rush to tell them something nice about themselves. People do that all the time even if they don't mean it and it drives me crazy. This is a process. Step by step. Stop. Let them know you have acknowledged their gift.

You are going to see the difference in people and start noticing how good they feel. Some people are givers. They want to give to you and you keep saying, "No. I don't want it."

God has been trying to give you something and you keep saying, "I am not worthy. I am not worthy."

Well, hello? What else is new? Of course, you are not worthy, but it doesn't matter because He delights in giving to you. He knows you are not worthy, He knows what you did last year, He knows what you did yesterday, and He still delights in giving to you. So, whenever God gives you something, I want you to practice this and say, "Oh my goodness! Thank you so much. I so appreciate that and I needed it."

Just take it. It is okay to take it. Be grateful. Be thankful.

The next thing you going to do is look at the person and find something to compliment. Anything – their hair, their watch, their nails – find anything. If they smell good say, "Oh my goodness! You smell good."

People love to hear praise and you never know what they are going through. Take a moment and say, "Oh my goodness! You have an amazing smile!" and keep on walking.

I am a drive-by compliment-giver. If I only have a few minutes, I am just going to say, "Oh, my gosh! I love all of that," or "That stuff right there, that's working. I love it," and keep going.

And I don't even know what happens next, but I do know they appreciate it because I know what it is like to be been down and need someone to give me a kind word, to acknowledge I exist, that I am here.

I want to encourage you in your relationships to give compliments from the heart. Don't expect anything in return, especially men. Don't think you are going to get away with murder. When you give a compliment and you start massaging her shoulders, she knows you want something. Don't wait until you need something to tell her how beautiful she is, how much you appreciate her, and how grateful you are that she is the mother of your children. Tell her she is fine and she is all that, when you don't need anything in return. If you wait to tell her she is amazing or that he is awesome when you want the credit card, they are going to know.

What else does Jeremiah say? *"Plans for peace and well-being and not for disaster..."*

Many of you are professional *what-if* scenario worriers. You can list everything that could possibly go wrong. You know what I am talking about. "Well, if I do that, this might happen. And if he says that, then I am going to say this. And then I am going to lose my job."

Oh my gosh! All I asked was, "How's your job?"

You have to stop being so negative, stop thinking about the what-ifs. Tomorrow was not promised to you, and when you obsess about the what-ifs then you lose your peace from today. You lose your peace worrying about something which may not even happen.

I have done it too but I don't do it anymore. I stay in the present because I know the thoughts and the plans He has for me are not for disaster. Pay attention to your language. Pay attention to the things you are saying because you know words have power.

I was watching to a video the other day which explained why NASCAR drivers don't put their focus on the wall. They drive right up next to it but they don't concentrate on it. If they started saying to themselves, "Don't hit the wall. Don't hit the wall. Don't hit the wall," do you know what would happen? Unconsciously, they would move the steering wheel little by little until they got close to the wall, and then boom!

Why don't you do what Ephesians says? Keep thinking about whatever is noble, whatever is good, whatever is kind. Why won't you think about all those awesome things? Change your mind and change your life. Change what you think about because God says He knows the thoughts and the plans He has for you and they are not for disaster. Why not anticipate good stuff? That is what I am doing right now.

I am already celebrating the husband God has for me and getting ready. I am anticipating, of course, that he is going to be all kinds of fine, a man of God, on purpose, and that he is going to have a love for God bigger than the love he has for me. I am anticipating that he has a calling, he wants to serve, and he wants to be the kind of man who when he dies, the Lord says, "Well done, good and faithful servant."

I am already celebrating and living a life worthy of a husband. The way I dress lets you know this because even though I believe I am fearfully and wonderfully made, I am not going out there showing all my stuff. I am dressing like a woman who is set apart. Any man who looks at my life right now is going to say, "That woman is set apart for someone. That woman is waiting for her husband."

I know it is going to happen because the Bible says, "I know the plans and the thoughts that I have for you."

He knows those plans and those thoughts and they are good. So I am anticipating blessings. I am anticipating favor.

Every day, I ask, "Who's going to bless me today? Who's going to be awesome to me today? Who's going to love on me today? What encouraging text am I going to get today?"

Those are my thoughts. That is the mind-set it takes to have a healthy relationship because a healthy relationship requires healthy people.

There is no such a thing as a perfect mate – I have to tell you right now – because *you are not* perfect. Your partner is not going to be perfect either, but God is going to provide you a person who is blessed and is also walking according to God's will. And you are going to be healthy. You are going to have the right mind-set. You are going to have the right attitude. And therefore, you are going to attract the right person because light attracts light. That is a fact. Amos 3:3 says, *"Will two walk together unless they agree?"*

So if you want an amazing wife or husband, and if you want your relationships to change, you have to become what you seek. I'll say that one more time. **If you want an amazing woman or man of God, *you* have to become an amazing man**

or woman of God. You cannot demand of somebody else what you are not willing to be yourself. There are so many people saying, "I want to have this amazing man of God," and they don't even go to church, open their Bible, or sit down to pray.

Do you think a healthy man or woman of God is going to look at you if you walk and don't have any fruit? They are not going to do that. They respect themselves. They know they have inside information. When you know you have inside information, you don't settle for anything less than what He has for you. You just can't.

A relationship is like going to a bakery. When you go to the bakery, they have a whole bunch of cakes there already made. You can walk up, grab one for yourself, and go in a couple of seconds. But, if you are choosy (and I am asking you to be choosy), you are going to walk up to the bakery counter and place an order. You are going to say, "I want a 5LB cake with butter icing. I want it to be purple with gold, and I want it to be square, not round. I want it to have flowers one on each corner and the flowers should be sunflowers – and not just any little sunflower, a big sunflower."

The baker is going to say, "That sounds like a great cake, but it's going to take me some time to make it for you."

Do you see where I am going? It is going to take some time to get that cake. Don't go up to the counter and grab any old cake. Stop doing that. Your cake takes time to bake. It is a big cake. It is a juicy, delicious cake, made to order just for you. But, you have to wait, my darling. My dear, you have to wait for that cake.

Trust me, when you get your hands on that cake......all bets are off because that cake is going to be **good**. You are going to say, "Guys, I am going to have to leave for a little bit. I need to enjoy me some cake right now."

You will enjoy that cake because it was made to order just for you. The Bible says, *"I know the plans and the thoughts I have for you."* He is the ultimate baker, thank you very much. He is putting together an amazing cake for you and for me. Why would you settle for a ready-made cake which has been sitting there for so long that nobody else wants it? Because you don't know Whose you are. You forget you have inside information.

What else does the Bible say? He says, *"Plans for peace and well-being and not for disaster, to give you a future and a hope."*

To give you a future – what does that mean? It means you are provided for, that you will have the resources you need to be all set in the future. God is saying, "I am giving you a future," and that future He has provided includes your relationships. **You just have to wait because** He is not building you any old relationship. It takes time. He has an amazing future for you – and that takes time. It is as simple as that. It takes time. My friends, my brothers, my sisters, He knows the plans and the thoughts He has for you.

"And hope" – hope is my favorite because hope is equal to faith. You are hoping and expecting that He has something amazing for you. **And I know He does**; I have no doubt in my mind. He continues to give to me, day in and day out. Did you know that when I ask Him for the right things, He provides? Have you noticed that too? When you ask God for the right thing, the right people, the right circumstances, He answers. You have to quit asking, "God, give me a million dollars. God, make me rich.

God, give me a woman so fine that everyone will be so jealous they won't be able to stand it. Give me a man so fine that when he puts on a suit, people have to stop and stare."

Why are you are asking for those things? What benefit does God get in that? How is He going to glorify Himself if He gives you those things?

However, when you say to God, "God, I am in a season of growth. Things are changing. I am going in a different direction. Can you and I chat for a set period of time? Can you tell me how you want me to do this? Can you tell me what direction you want me to take? Can you show me your plan because I want to walk only within your will? I only want to do those things you want me to do," do you know what God says?

"Of course," because He's awesome like that. "Of course, we can spend quality time together."

He is a jealous God. He wants to squeeze you up. He wants to kiss you. He wants to smell you up, even early in the morning, spend time with you and say, "I love you so much" because He does.

You have to change the quality of your questions. You must. And you have to have faith that He will do it. And that's hope – hope is faith that He will do it.

The calling you have, not anyone can do it. You know that right? I hope you do. The calling you have has your first name, your middle name, your last name and all your fingerprints all over it. You are unique. There was a unique recipe He put in the mold when He made you that has your calling encoded on it. Your calling requires you to dress apart. It requires you to show up looking all kinds of fine. Your calling requires you to accept gifts and to live a life of expectation.

When you are invited to a party you are sent an invitation. When I was doing my *TEDx* talk, even though I was booked to speak, I got an invitation. I got dressed up as I love to do, showed up at the appointed time and place, knowing I was going to get in. I dressed, I drove, I took the time, I prepared and I did my part. The rest was up to someone else. The rest is up to Him, but you must do your part.

My words for 2016 are: ready, available, and servant. You know what I do? I get up, take a shower, take care of my hair and makeup, I dress up, I drive and I show up. I say: Where do you want me to go? Where do I set the GPS for? It doesn't matter where you want me to go, I am going there period.

For your relationships, there is a GPS called His will for your life. If you are serious about your relationships, if you are spending time and money to get ready and right, you are going to turn on that GPS. The GOD GPS is ready for you – His GPS never gets lost, never loses signal, and never sends you around a corner when you are supposed to go straight. His GPS is always right. And even when you think you are lost, everything works together for good for those who love Him and are called according to His will. So, you have to take a few detours. Who hasn't? I know I have, but that is okay. I am not late. You are not late. Stop looking at the clock. The clock has messed with so many people, it is not even funny. I want you to stop that right now in the Name of Jesus. You are not late.

"But, Catherine, I want to have children. But, Catherine, I want to buy a house. But, Catherine, I..."

Stop it! Stop it right now. The clock is not your enemy. The clock is your friend. Remember, you are putting in an order and that order is going to turn up perfect. You know it is, but you are going to have to stop looking at the clock and saying, "But, God, I am going to get him because even though he is missing an eye and a leg, you know, he's a Christian sort of so I am going to grab him."

What? Stop looking at the clock. You have all the time in the world. What He has for you is for waiting for you – He has set it aside for you. Remember, He's never late. He's right on time, but you have to be ready and be available.

When you are on Skype and you want to talk to someone in a different time zone, their little button turns green when they are available. I love that! It is a metaphor for life. I want your green light to be on all the time.

When you see big city cabs with their lights off, you know they aren't free to pick up passengers. I don't want you to ever turn off your light. Don't worry about how you are going to do it, or not do it, don't worry about anything. He has already made a way.

Do you remember when Jesus was getting ready to enter Jerusalem before His crucifixion and He needed a donkey? Wasn't the donkey already provided?

Wasn't the donkey already where it was supposed to be, and the person who was going to give it knew that they had to give it? Come on! He has provided already, but you have to be ready, available and willing to serve. **You have to. You must.**

Your relationships have to be according to Jeremiah 29:11, *"For I know the plans I have for you, says the Lord – plans for peace and well-being and not for disaster, to give you a future and a hope."*

When you make that scripture the cornerstone of your life, your relationships are going to change and you are going to change. My brothers and my sister, this is what I wanted to share with you. I hope you take advantage of this teaching because many of you complain, "Nobody gives to me. Nobody tells me anything. God is quiet. I don't know what to do."

You don't have those excuses anymore because God has spoken to you. He has told you exactly what to do, how to do it, when to do it. The only question now is: Are you going to do it? Are you going to listen? Are you going to be like the man who built his house on the rock? He built his house on the rock because he knew that was exactly what he needed to do.

That is how you have good relationships, my friends. That is the *only* way to have good relationships, the only way. I hope you listen. I hope you live a life of expectation, expecting that He who promised is faithful.

Make sure you say hello in social media via @StyleStoring or visit us at www.StylingFaith.Com